EMMANUEL JOSEPH

The Restructuring Toolkit: Bouncing Back Stronger after Sack

Copyright © 2025 by Emmanuel Joseph

All rights reserved. No part of this publication may be reproduced, stored or transmitted in any form or by any means, electronic, mechanical, photocopying, recording, scanning, or otherwise without written permission from the publisher. It is illegal to copy this book, post it to a website, or distribute it by any other means without permission.

First edition

This book was professionally typeset on Reedsy. Find out more at reedsy.com

Contents

1	Chapter 1	1
2	Chapter 1: The Initial Shock	4
3	Chapter 2: Understanding the Reasons	6
4	Chapter 3: Self-Assessment and Reflection	8
5	Chapter 4: Building a Strong Resume and LinkedIn Profile	10
6	Chapter 5: Networking and Building Relationships	12
7	Chapter 6: Upgrading Your Skills	14
8	Chapter 7: Preparing for Interviews	15
9	Chapter 8: Negotiating Job Offers	17
10	Chapter 9: Embracing a Growth Mindset	19
11	Chapter 10: Balancing Work and Life	21
12	Chapter 11: Staying Motivated and Positive	23
13	Chapter 12: Building a Resilient Career	25

1

Chapter 1

Introduction: The Restructuring Toolkit: Bouncing Back Stronger after Sack

In today's fast-paced world, job security can often feel like a distant dream. Economic fluctuations, technological advancements, and shifting corporate priorities mean that even the most dedicated employees can face the sudden and jarring experience of being laid off. It's a moment that many dread, yet few are truly prepared for. This book aims to provide a lifeline for those navigating this difficult period, offering practical advice, emotional support, and actionable strategies to help you bounce back stronger than ever.

Losing a job is more than just a financial blow; it can shake your confidence, disrupt your daily routine, and leave you questioning your self-worth. It's a situation that can feel overwhelmingly personal, even though it is often a result of broader organizational changes. Recognizing that you are not alone in this experience is the first step toward recovery. This book is here to remind you that many have faced similar challenges and have emerged not just intact, but thriving.

The initial shock of losing your job can be paralyzing. The days and weeks that follow may be filled with uncertainty and fear, making it difficult to see a path forward. However, this period of upheaval can also be a catalyst for growth and reinvention. By embracing the change and viewing it as an opportunity rather than a setback, you can begin to build a new and more resilient career. This book will guide you through this transformation, offering tools and insights to help you turn adversity into advantage.

One of the most important aspects of bouncing back from a job loss is understanding the reasons behind it. Whether it's due to company restructuring, economic downturns, or performance issues, gaining clarity on the factors that led to your dismissal can provide valuable insights for your next steps. This book will help you conduct a thorough self-assessment, identify areas for improvement, and develop a plan to address them. By learning from the past, you can pave the way for a brighter future.

A key component of your recovery journey will be building a strong personal brand. In today's competitive job market, it's not enough to simply have a resume; you need to showcase your unique strengths and accomplishments in a way that sets you apart. This book will provide practical tips on crafting a compelling resume and LinkedIn profile, as well as strategies for networking and building relationships. By presenting yourself confidently and effectively, you can attract the right opportunities and make a powerful impression on potential employers.

The process of bouncing back also involves upgrading your skills and staying relevant in your field. The rapid pace of technological change means that continuous learning is essential for career success. This book will guide you through identifying the skills that are in demand, exploring online courses and certifications, and seeking out practical experiences that can enhance your expertise. By committing to lifelong learning, you can stay ahead of industry trends and remain a valuable asset in any organization.

Resilience is not just about finding a new job; it's about building a sustainable and fulfilling career. This book emphasizes the importance of maintaining a growth mindset, staying motivated, and achieving a healthy work-life balance. By setting clear goals, managing your time effectively, and prioritizing self-care, you can create a career that is not only successful but also aligned with your values and passions. This holistic approach will help you navigate future challenges with confidence and grace.

Finally, this book is a testament to the power of the human spirit. It serves

CHAPTER 1

as a reminder that you are capable of overcoming adversity and achieving greatness, even in the face of significant setbacks. By leveraging the tools and strategies provided in these pages, you can transform a challenging experience into an opportunity for growth and renewal. The journey ahead may be difficult, but with resilience, determination, and the right support, you can bounce back stronger than ever before.

2

Chapter 1: The Initial Shock

Losing a job can feel like an earth-shattering event, shaking the foundation of one's life. It's a moment where emotions like disbelief, anger, and fear swirl together in a tempest. Understanding that these feelings are natural and that you are not alone in this journey is crucial. This chapter explores the initial shock and provides tools to help ground yourself during this turbulent time. Accepting the reality of the situation is the first step towards healing and bouncing back stronger.

Acknowledging the emotional rollercoaster is essential. It's okay to grieve the loss of your job, but it's equally important to set a time limit on this grief. Giving yourself permission to feel, followed by a conscious decision to move forward, will prevent you from getting stuck in a cycle of despair. Reaching out to friends and family can provide a support system that is invaluable during this period.

The shock of job loss often comes with a sense of identity crisis. For many, their profession is a significant part of who they are. This chapter guides you through the process of re-evaluating your self-worth and finding your identity beyond your job. Engaging in activities that you enjoy and excel at can help restore your sense of self.

It's also important to take care of your physical health during this time. Stress can take a toll on your body, so maintaining a routine that includes exercise, a balanced diet, and adequate sleep is vital. These practices not only help manage stress but also boost your overall well-being, making you more resilient.

Lastly, this chapter emphasizes the importance of seeking professional help if needed. Whether it's career counseling or therapy, professional guidance can provide you with the tools and perspective necessary to navigate this challenging period. Remember, asking for help is a sign of strength, not weakness.

3

Chapter 2: Understanding the Reasons

Understanding why you were let go is a critical part of the healing process. This chapter delves into the common reasons for job loss, whether it's company restructuring, financial instability, or performance-related issues. By gaining clarity on the reasons, you can start to form a plan for moving forward and avoid making the same mistakes in the future.

Company restructuring is a frequent cause of job loss, and it's often beyond your control. Understanding the market dynamics and the company's financial health can provide insights into why certain decisions were made. This knowledge can also help you identify industries or sectors that are more stable and better aligned with your career goals.

Performance-related issues can be tough to swallow, but they offer a valuable opportunity for growth. This chapter provides strategies for honest self-assessment and ways to seek constructive feedback. Embracing a growth mindset and viewing mistakes as learning opportunities can help you develop the skills needed for future success.

If your job loss was due to financial instability within the company, it's essential to understand the broader economic context. This chapter guides you through analyzing market trends and economic indicators that may have contributed to your situation. Armed with this knowledge, you can make more informed decisions about your next career move.

CHAPTER 2: UNDERSTANDING THE REASONS

Legal and ethical considerations are also discussed in this chapter. Knowing your rights as an employee can help you navigate the aftermath of job loss. This includes understanding severance packages, unemployment benefits, and non-compete clauses. Being informed empowers you to make decisions that are in your best interest.

4

Chapter 3: Self-Assessment and Reflection

Self-assessment is a crucial step in bouncing back from job loss. This chapter provides tools and exercises to help you reflect on your career, skills, and passions. By understanding your strengths and areas for improvement, you can chart a path that aligns with your true self and career aspirations.

Begin by conducting a thorough inventory of your skills and accomplishments. This chapter offers techniques for identifying transferable skills that can open up new career opportunities. Understanding what you bring to the table boosts your confidence and helps you articulate your value to potential employers.

Reflecting on your career path so far is another important exercise. This chapter guides you through evaluating your past roles, achievements, and challenges. By analyzing what has worked well and what hasn't, you can gain insights into the type of work environment and responsibilities that suit you best.

Passion and purpose play a significant role in career satisfaction. This chapter includes exercises to help you identify what you are truly passionate about and how to align your career with your purpose. Pursuing work that resonates with your values and interests can lead to greater fulfillment and long-term success.

Setting clear and achievable goals is the next step in the self-assessment process. This chapter provides strategies for defining your short-term and long-term career goals. By breaking down these goals into actionable steps, you can create a roadmap that guides your job search and career development.

5

Chapter 4: Building a Strong Resume and LinkedIn Profile

A well-crafted resume and LinkedIn profile are essential tools in your job search. This chapter offers tips and templates for creating documents that stand out to recruiters and hiring managers. By highlighting your achievements and skills effectively, you can make a compelling case for why you are the right fit for the job.

Start with a clear and concise summary that showcases your professional identity. This chapter provides guidance on writing a powerful summary that captures the essence of your career and sets the tone for the rest of your resume. Tailoring your summary to each job application can increase your chances of getting noticed.

Quantifying your achievements is a key strategy in making your resume stand out. This chapter offers techniques for showcasing your accomplishments with specific metrics and examples. By demonstrating the impact you've had in previous roles, you can build a strong case for your potential value to a new employer.

Your LinkedIn profile is a dynamic representation of your professional brand. This chapter includes tips for optimizing your profile, from writing a compelling headline to crafting a detailed and engaging summary. By leveraging the platform's features, you can increase your visibility and connect with potential employers and industry professionals.

Networking is another crucial aspect of your LinkedIn strategy. This chapter provides advice on building and maintaining professional relationships online. By engaging with your network and sharing valuable content, you can position yourself as a thought leader in your field and uncover hidden job opportunities.

6

Chapter 5: Networking and Building Relationships

Networking is a powerful tool in your job search. This chapter explores the importance of building and nurturing professional relationships, both online and offline. By expanding your network, you can gain access to opportunities and insights that can accelerate your career recovery.

Start by reconnecting with former colleagues, mentors, and industry contacts. This chapter provides tips on how to reach out and rekindle professional relationships. Genuine and thoughtful communication can open doors and provide valuable support during your job search.

Attending industry events and conferences is another effective way to expand your network. This chapter offers strategies for making the most of these events, from preparing your elevator pitch to following up with new connections. By actively participating in your professional community, you can stay informed and discover new opportunities.

Building relationships online is equally important. This chapter includes advice on engaging with industry groups and forums, participating in webinars, and leveraging social media. By sharing your expertise and insights, you can establish yourself as a valuable member of your professional community.

CHAPTER 5: NETWORKING AND BUILDING RELATIONSHIPS

Informational interviews are a valuable tool for learning about potential career paths and gaining insights from industry experts. This chapter guides you through the process of requesting and conducting informational interviews. By asking thoughtful questions and showing genuine interest, you can build meaningful connections and gather valuable information.

7

Chapter 6: Upgrading Your Skills

In a constantly evolving job market, upgrading your skills is essential. This chapter explores the importance of continuous learning and provides strategies for identifying and acquiring the skills needed to stay competitive. By investing in your professional development, you can enhance your employability and career prospects.

Begin by conducting a skills gap analysis. This chapter offers techniques for assessing your current skills and identifying areas for improvement. By understanding the skills in demand in your industry, you can focus your efforts on acquiring the most relevant and valuable competencies.

Online courses and certifications are a convenient and effective way to upgrade your skills. This chapter includes recommendations for reputable platforms and resources that offer high-quality training. By committing to lifelong learning, you can stay ahead of industry trends and advancements.

Practical experience is equally important in developing new skills. This chapter provides advice on seeking internships, volunteer opportunities, and freelance projects. Gaining hands-on experience can help you apply your knowledge and build a portfolio that showcases your capabilities.

Mentorship is another valuable aspect of skill development. This chapter guides you through the process of finding and working with a mentor. By seeking guidance and feedback from experienced professionals, you can accelerate your learning and gain valuable insights into your chosen field.

8

Chapter 7: Preparing for Interviews

Interviews are a crucial step in the job search process. This chapter provides tips and techniques for preparing and excelling in interviews. By presenting yourself confidently and effectively, you can make a positive impression on potential employers and increase your chances of landing the job.

Start by researching the company and the role you are applying for. This chapter offers strategies for gathering information and understanding the company's culture, values, and goals. Being well-informed demonstrates your genuine interest and helps you tailor your responses to align with the company's needs.

Practicing common interview questions is another important preparation step. This chapter includes a list of frequently asked questions and provides guidance on crafting thoughtful and concise answers. By rehearsing your responses, you can articulate your skills and experiences clearly and confidently.

Behavioral interviews are common in many industries, and this chapter offers techniques for mastering this interview style. Using the STAR method (Situation, Task, Action, Result), you can structure your answers to highlight your problem-solving abilities and accomplishments. Providing specific examples and quantifiable results can make your responses more compelling.

First impressions matter, and this chapter includes tips on making a positive impact from the moment you walk into the interview room. From dressing appropriately to maintaining good body language, small details can influence the interviewer's perception of you. Being polite, professional, and enthusiastic throughout the interview can leave a lasting impression.

9

Chapter 8: Negotiating Job Offers

Once you start receiving job offers, it's important to approach negotiations with confidence and knowledge. This chapter provides strategies for evaluating and negotiating job offers to ensure that you secure a role that meets your needs and aligns with your career goals.

Begin by assessing the entire compensation package, not just the salary. This chapter offers guidance on evaluating benefits such as health insurance, retirement plans, and vacation time. Understanding the full value of the offer can help you make a more informed decision.

Researching industry standards and salary ranges for your role is essential. This chapter includes tips for gathering market data and determining a fair salary range. Armed with this information, you can negotiate more effectively and confidently.

Preparing for the negotiation process is key. This chapter provides techniques for practicing your negotiation skills and developing persuasive arguments. By clearly articulating your value and the reasons for your requested compensation, you can increase your chances of a successful negotiation.

Flexibility and compromise are also important in negotiations. This chapter offers advice on identifying non-salary benefits that are important to you and being open to trade-offs. Finding a win-win solution can help you build a positive relationship with your new employer from the start.

Lastly, this chapter emphasizes the importance of getting the final offer in writing. Understanding the terms and conditions of your employment agreement can prevent misunderstandings and ensure that both parties are clear on the expectations and commitments.

10

Chapter 9: Embracing a Growth Mindset

A growth mindset is essential for long-term career success and resilience. This chapter explores the principles of a growth mindset and provides strategies for cultivating this mindset in your professional and personal life.

Understanding the difference between a fixed mindset and a growth mindset is the first step. This chapter explains how a growth mindset embraces challenges, learns from feedback, and views effort as a path to mastery. By adopting this perspective, you can approach your career with a sense of curiosity and a willingness to learn.

Embracing failure as a learning opportunity is a key aspect of a growth mindset. This chapter offers techniques for reframing setbacks and viewing them as valuable experiences. By analyzing what went wrong and how you can improve, you can develop resilience and a proactive approach to challenges.

Continuous learning and skill development are central to a growth mindset. This chapter provides tips for staying curious and seeking out new knowledge and experiences. By committing to lifelong learning, you can stay adaptable and prepared for changes in the job market.

Setting goals and tracking progress are important for maintaining a growth mindset. This chapter includes strategies for defining clear and achievable goals, as well as methods for monitoring your progress and celebrating milestones. By staying focused and motivated, you can achieve your career aspirations.

11

Chapter 10: Balancing Work and Life

Achieving a healthy work-life balance is crucial for long-term well-being and career satisfaction. This chapter explores the importance of balance and provides strategies for managing your time and energy effectively.

Understanding your priorities is the first step to achieving balance. This chapter offers techniques for identifying what matters most to you in both your professional and personal life. By aligning your activities with your values, you can create a more fulfilling and balanced lifestyle.

Time management is a critical skill for maintaining balance. This chapter provides tips for planning your day, setting boundaries, and avoiding burnout. By prioritizing tasks and delegating when necessary, you can ensure that you have time for both work and personal activities.

Self-care is an essential aspect of work-life balance. This chapter emphasizes the importance of taking care of your physical, mental, and emotional health. Incorporating practices such as exercise, mindfulness, and relaxation into your routine can help you stay resilient and focused.

Building supportive relationships is also important for balance. This chapter includes advice on nurturing your personal and professional connections. By maintaining a strong support network, you can navigate challenges more effectively and enjoy a more enriched life.

Flexibility and adaptability are key to achieving and maintaining balance.

THE RESTRUCTURING TOOLKIT: BOUNCING BACK STRONGER AFTER SACK

This chapter offers strategies for adjusting your approach as your circumstances change. By staying open to new possibilities and being willing to make adjustments, you can maintain a balanced and fulfilling life.

12

Chapter 11: Staying Motivated and Positive

Staying motivated and positive during a job search and beyond is crucial for success. This chapter provides strategies for maintaining a positive attitude and staying motivated throughout your career journey.

Setting realistic and achievable goals is a key aspect of staying motivated. This chapter offers techniques for breaking down larger goals into manageable steps and celebrating your progress along the way. By focusing on small wins, you can maintain momentum and stay motivated.

Maintaining a positive attitude is equally important. This chapter provides tips for cultivating a positive mindset, such as practicing gratitude, surrounding yourself with positive influences, and focusing on your strengths. By staying optimistic, you can navigate challenges more effectively and stay resilient.

Building a routine and sticking to it can help maintain motivation. This chapter includes advice on creating a daily schedule that includes time for job search activities, self-care, and relaxation. By establishing a routine, you can stay organized and focused.

Seeking support from others is another important strategy. This chapter emphasizes the value of connecting with friends, family, and professional networks. By sharing your experiences and receiving encouragement and advice, you can stay motivated and feel less isolated.

Lastly, this chapter highlights the importance of staying adaptable and open to new opportunities. Embracing change and being willing to pivot when necessary can help you stay motivated and open to new possibilities.

13

Chapter 12: Building a Resilient Career

Building a resilient career is about more than just bouncing back from job loss; it's about creating a sustainable and fulfilling professional life. This chapter explores the principles of career resilience and provides strategies for long-term success.

Understanding the importance of adaptability is key to career resilience. This chapter explains how staying flexible and open to change can help you navigate the ups and downs of your career. By continuously learning and evolving, you can stay relevant and prepared for new opportunities.

Networking and relationship-building are critical for a resilient career. This chapter provides tips for maintaining and expanding your professional network. By building strong connections, you can access new opportunities, gain insights, and receive support throughout your career.

Maintaining a growth mindset is another important aspect of career resilience. This chapter emphasizes the value of staying curious, seeking feedback, and embracing challenges. By cultivating a growth mindset, you can continuously improve and stay motivated.

Taking care of your well-being is essential for long-term career success. This chapter includes advice on prioritizing your physical, mental, and emotional health. By maintaining a balanced and healthy lifestyle, you can stay energized and focused on your career goals.

Finally, this chapter encourages you to reflect on your career journey and celebrate your achievements. By recognizing your successes and learning from your experiences, you can build a fulfilling and resilient career.

Book Description: The Restructuring Toolkit: Bouncing Back Stronger after Sack

In a world where job security is no longer guaranteed, "The Restructuring Toolkit: Bouncing Back Stronger after Sack" is your essential guide to navigating the challenges of job loss and emerging stronger and more resilient. This comprehensive book provides practical advice, emotional support, and actionable strategies to help you turn the setback of losing a job into an opportunity for growth and reinvention.

From understanding the initial shock and emotional impact of being laid off to conducting a thorough self-assessment and reflecting on your career, this book covers every aspect of the journey to recovery. Learn how to build a compelling resume and LinkedIn profile, master the art of networking and building professional relationships, and upgrade your skills to stay competitive in an ever-evolving job market.

"The Restructuring Toolkit" also emphasizes the importance of maintaining a growth mindset, staying motivated, and achieving a healthy work-life balance. With chapters dedicated to preparing for interviews, negotiating job offers, and building a resilient career, this book equips you with the tools and insights needed to succeed in your professional life.

Filled with practical tips, real-life examples, and expert advice, "The Restructuring Toolkit" is more than just a guide to finding a new job—it's a roadmap to creating a sustainable and fulfilling career. Whether you're facing job loss for the first time or looking to bounce back from a setback, this book will inspire and empower you to take charge of your future and achieve your career goals.